souls.

Umm Zakiyyah

souls.
by Umm Zakiyyah

Copyright © 2018 by Al-Walaa Publications.
All Rights Reserved.

ISBN: 978-1-942985-18-1

Order information at **uzauthor.com/bookstore**

Published by Al-Walaa Publications
Gwynn Oak, Maryland USA

from the journal of
Umm Zakiyyah

There are no good or bad people in the world, at least not in the absolute sense. There are only sinful people who repent and sinful people who do not repent. It is the presence or absence of repentance that makes a person righteous or corrupt, not the presence or absence of *sin.*

When we teach our children to put God first, we need to understand that this means He comes before even us. And while this means they will, *bi'idhnillah*, hold on to their faith throughout their lives, it also means they'll sometimes make life decisions that we neither understand nor agree with. And if this disturbs us more than the alternative—seeking to control their thoughts and choices—then we need to teach ourselves the same lesson we taught our *children*.

No fault or sin of yours is bigger than God's mercy and *forgiveness.*

God doesn't ask for perfect souls. He asks for believing souls, and repentant *ones.*

Keep going.
Your "small" efforts are significant to

Those for whom this world is a Paradise will always see worldly success as a direct reflection of your personal work ethic, inherent goodness, and motivation. Don't make the same mistake. You might enjoy some comforts in this earthly prison, but in the end, prison is still prison. And there's no inherent goodness in earning "success" in a prison—unless it ultimately earns you absolution and release. And for the believer, that absolution is God's forgiveness, and that release is

Jannah.

You can't compete with self-hate. If someone doesn't love themselves, they can't love *you.*

Self-love is putting your mental, emotional, and spiritual health above all else. It is recognizing your ever-present susceptibility to falling into self-deception, error, and sin. Thus, self-love is manifested in the creating of healthy boundaries, which protect the self from the harm of others, but most importantly from the harm of *self.*

You can't master patience without gratefulness, and you can't master gratefulness without *patience.*

Too often we suffer continuously and label it "patience" or "gratefulness" because it is too painful to face the truth of who or what inflicted our deepest wounds. But denial does not bring healing. It brings only deeper wounds and prolonged *suffering.*

I think our enemies are sent to beautify our hearts, fortify our spirits, and cleanse our *souls.*

We have to be better at taking responsibility for our actions—and for respecting the right of others to their *own*.

my Lord,
forgive me
I have wronged my soul.
my Lord,
pardon me
I have forgotten myself.
O my Lord,
guide me
and help me
to help my soul
to help me
find *You.*

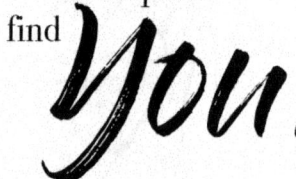

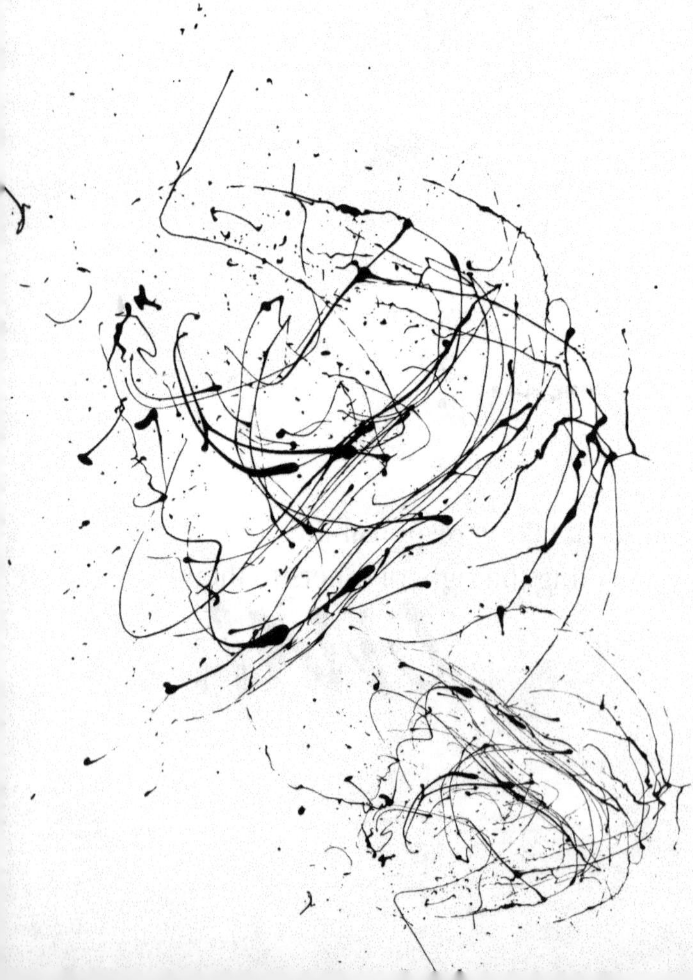

what happens to a soul deterred?
does it get covered up
like the lifeless in the ground?
or does it wander like the blind and deaf
who see no light and hear no sound?
or does it rot like a corpse
in the desert heat?
lying still—
an abandoned heap.
maybe it just gives up
like it's told
or does it *implode?*

You don't have to save the world.
You just have to save your soul.
Then Paradise is *yours.*

I don't know if I've met believers more beautiful than those who guard their tongues, assume the best about others, and refrain from having opinions about matters that don't concern *them.*

I washed the flames
from my skin
then
fought the fire *within.*

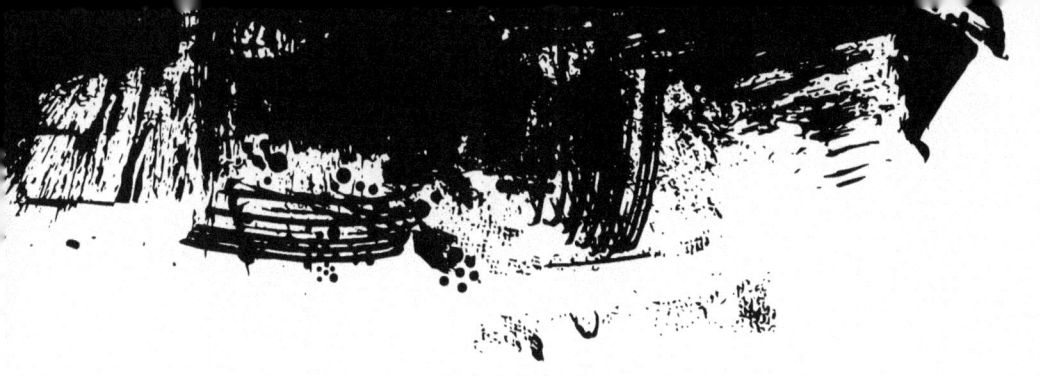

Allow me this moment to cry,
for my heart is heavy in pain.
Allow me, dear soul, this moment to grieve.
For I have burdens only my Lord can *relieve.*

blind faith.
I know no faith
blinder
than that
which promises nothing.
but a bed of dirt—
at best.
and eternal torment
at *worst.*

What are you most afraid of during these difficult times? If the answer does not include the state of your heart and soul, then the problems that loom before you are much bigger and more destructive than the ones you fear *most.*

Problems are like energy.
They never go away completely.
They just change form,
direction,
and *intensity*.

It's a beautiful feeling when you feel grateful
for all that God has given you. And I don't
mean from that obligatory sense of knowing
that being thankful is the right thing to do.
I mean from a genuine place of happiness
in your heart—when you look at all the
blessings and challenges in your life,
all the happiness and pain, and
all the moments you couldn't imagine things
getting any worse.
Yet you know deep inside,
"Don't worry. He's got this. It's your
customized path to Paradise,
if you choose to walk in His *way.*"

I'm learning to see the good in this trial. Patience and gratefulness are the lessons I am learning from all of the pain and confusion in the world—and in my *soul.*

Quieting the restless soul is one of the most difficult trials in *life.*

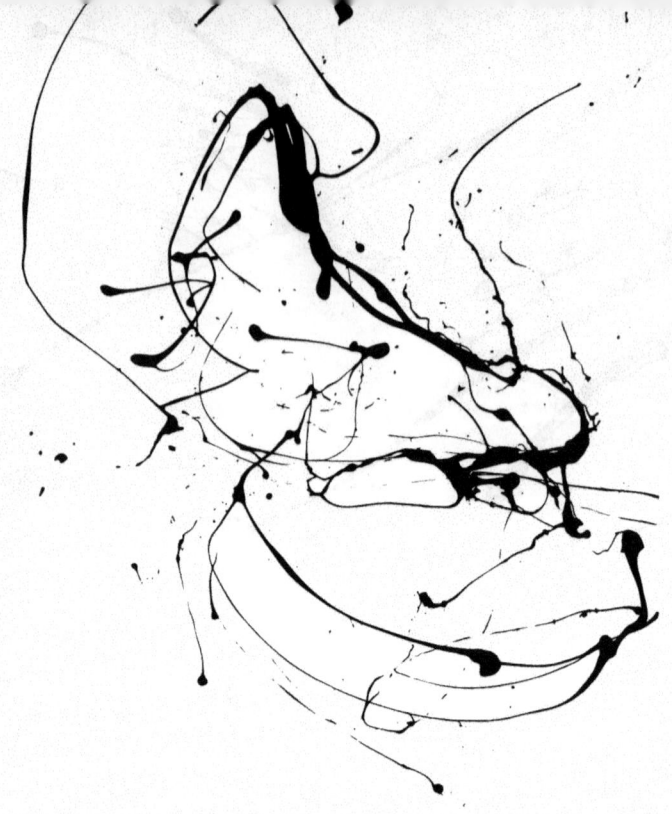

Acknowledge the pain. Don't live in the pain.
But be present with it.
Then let it pass through *you.*

I travel light
and I travel alone
carrying only my *emaan*–
that spiritual light of faith
that illuminates the *heart.*

Soul connections are real and divinely *decreed.*

Pain is part of the pleasure.
The agony of adversity fuels the tranquil sweetness of ease.
So be patient. Then be grateful.
For the affair of the believer is always *good.*

I think the point is humility.
Not toxic shame, not self-hate,
and certainly not perfection.
Just sincere humility.
This is why we sin.
This is why not a single one of us is innocent.
This is why not a single one of us is without a battle we're fighting. Some privately, some publicly, some both.
And that's the point.
We can never escape our humanity.
And we're not supposed *to.*

But we cannot submit to sin.
We cannot submit to disbelief.
This is how we lose the battle.
And we should never give up the battle.
Triumph is in never giving up,
not in having no battle to *fight.*

The battlefield is our spirit-soul,
and that's why it hurts so much.
That's why it's so much easier to just give up.
To pretend that the battle is already won.
Or that we should have no battle to fight.
Or that the battle is always "out there"
in the sins of someone else's *life.*

"But what's the point?" we sometimes ask in frustration.
And I get it.
I've asked myself this question on many an occasion,
especially when I doubted my ability
to hold on to my faith.
Why give us tests we won't pass, sins we'll continuously fall into,
and desires we can never fulfill?
I certainly cannot speak on behalf of God,
so let me speak on behalf of myself.
I think the point is  *humility.*

Even when we're getting everything right with all the do's and don'ts, we often fall prey to one of the worst crimes against the spirit-soul.
Kibr.
That destructive pride that makes you look down on others and reject the truth.
And I don't mean only "truth" as in what is listed as right or wrong in Divine Scripture, but truth as in what is written as right or wrong in our own prideful ways—
and tormented *souls.*

The wilderness of the soul doesn't come with
a customized roadmap.
But you've got to get through it anyway,
battling all the unruly wildlife and hungry beasts
that threaten your spiritual
and emotional safety
along the
way.

I've learned to find peace in my own company. But there's nothing glamorous about staying true to yourself. Sometimes not a single soul understands your path. So you have to make peace with the solitude of knowing your *Lord.*

If you're going to move forward in life,
you have to embrace the struggle and hurt
like you embrace the blessings and happiness.
No, I don't mean you rejoice during struggles
and hardship, and I don't mean you should like to hurt.
But embrace the full spectrum of what life means.
And when things get hard, bear the difficulty patiently
and seek the lesson in it—
and that better part of
yourself.

If you want to master life, then master two things: patience and gratitude.
When you are in difficulty, confusion, or distress, cling to patience.
When you are in ease, happiness, and comfort, cling to *gratitude.*

Patience and gratefulness.
They are two halves of a whole,
and each is the heart of the *other.*

True faith isn't about walking through life completely happy and undisturbed in every circumstance. It's about staying sincerely connected to your Lord despite the inevitable ups and downs in *life.*

But giving your problems to your Creator and having *tawakkul*—complete trust in Him—is not always a smooth, tranquil process.
 When you're really stressed out, hurt, or confused, you don't always feel good or a sense of peace right away, even if you're constantly praying and asking for *guidance.*

Many times, the process of *tawakkul* continues to be an internal battle for a very long time. But this isn't a sign of weak faith. It's a sign of the natural fragility of the human heart— and a sign of the believing soul seeking *purity*.

Having true faith and trust in God isn't about perfection. It's about remaining in sincere remembrance of your Lord and in humble obedience to Him, whether you're enjoying times of ease and happiness or enduring times of tremendous pain and *difficulty*.

If God chooses to test you with something, you're going to be tested with that. Whether it's a difficult marriage, an unexpected divorce, loss of wealth, or even spiritual trials. If it's written for you, it will be part of your life path—no matter how many "precautions" you take, whom you trust for "expert" or spiritual advice, or even how much you pray for guidance

beforehand.

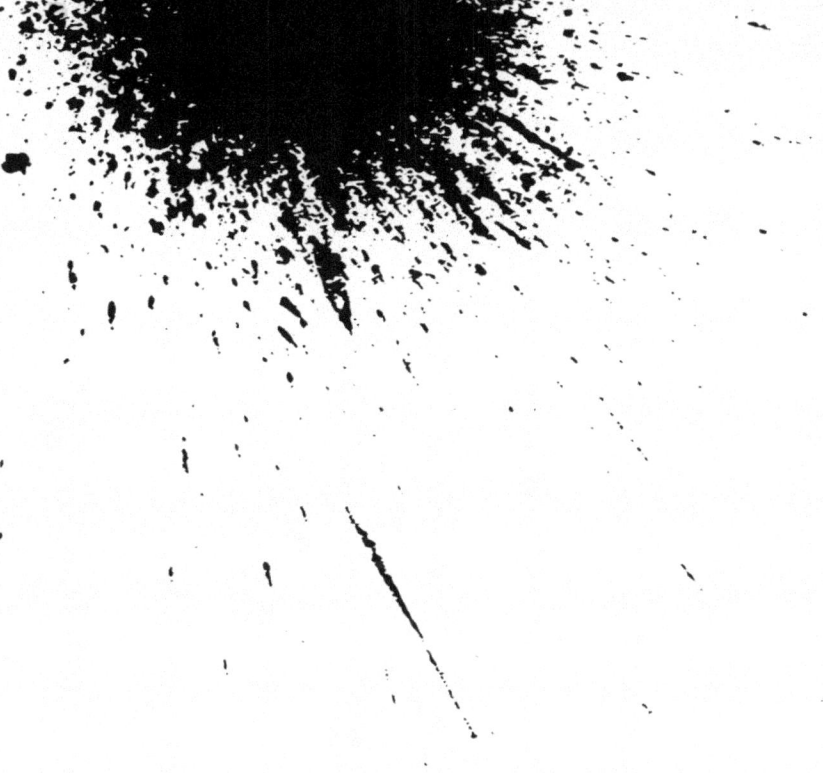

Trials are a part of life, and no one can escape them. But we still turn to God in prayerful supplication and *Istikhaarah*—seeking divine guidance before walking any path in life.
    This, so that our hearts can rest assured that whatever trial is befalling us is ultimately good for our life and soul, no matter how painful and confusing things are right *now*.

Instant gratification can become an addiction.
Beware of it affecting your faith and spirituality.
Everything good and beneficial doesn't
always feel good right away.
Sometimes it never
feels good right *away.*

But we don't do what is right and necessary because it feels good. We do what is right and necessary because it is right and *necessary.*

No matter how much knowledge we have, our greatest asset is our sincerity—to ourselves and others. And there is no sincerity without humility, no matter how convinced we are of our spiritual knowledge and good *intentions.*

The most any of us can hope for is God's mercy,
so when someone you admire
or greatly benefit from
falls into error or sin,
do not feel disappointed or betrayed.
Rather feel grateful that you now can give back
to them—by raising your hands in supplication
and asking God to have mercy on *Them.*

We must rise above the pain, and take responsibility for our own souls.
No one can do that for *you.*

I think disappointment in people is a mercy from God.
It's a reminder that we've lost focus
 and raised creation above the status
that God has written for them.
And in the process, we forgot
where real greatness
comes from—
 God *alone.*

A true spiritual teacher is interested only in
enhancing your spiritual knowledge
so that you continuously improve
your relationship with your Creator,
fulfill your purpose on earth,
and ultimately enter Paradise.
Whether or not you gain this knowledge from
that teacher specifically is completely irrelevant,
as his or her primary concern is
the salvation of your soul
and your access to
authentic spirituality—
no matter where
or from whom
you are blessed to find *it.*

The greatest act of selflessness is
to put your soul before anything else—
including
and most especially *yourself.*

About the Author

Umm Zakiyyah is the bestselling author of more than twenty books, including the *If I Should Speak* trilogy and the self-help books *Reverencing the Wombs That Broke You* and *The Abuse of Forgiveness*.

She writes about the interfaith struggles of Muslims and Christians and the intercultural, spiritual, and moral struggles of Muslims in America. Her work has earned praise from writers, professors, and filmmakers and has been translated into multiple languages.

Her novel *His Other Wife* is now a short film.

To learn more about the author, visit **uzauthor.com**

Also By Umm Zakiyyah

If I Should Speak
A Voice
Footsteps
Realities of Submission
Hearts We Lost
The Friendship Promise
Muslim Girl
His Other Wife
UZ Short Story Collection
The Test Paper (a children's book)
Pain. From the Journal of Umm Zakiyyah
Broken yet Faithful. From the Journal of Umm Zakiyyah
Faith. From the Journal of Umm Zakiyyah
Let's Talk About Sex and Muslim Love
Reverencing the Wombs That Broke You: A Daughter of Rape and Abuse Inspires Healing and Healthy Family
And Then I Gave Up: Essays About Faith and Spiritual Crisis in Islam
I Almost Left Islam: How I Reclaimed My Faith
The Abuse of Forgiveness: Manipulation and Harm in the Name of Emotional Healing
even if.
No One Taught Me the Human Side of Islam: The Muslim Hippie's Story of Living with Bipolar Disorder
The Month of Mercy, Not Perfection: A Ramadan Journal

Order information at **uzauthor.com/bookstore**

www.ingramcontent.com/pod-product-compliance
Lightning Source LLC
Chambersburg PA
CBHW070858050426
42453CB00012B/2259

The Unveiled

Rediscovering the Zadokite Covenant of the First 3000

Dr. Miles R. Jones
Patrick J. McGuire

© Copyright 2025 Miles R. Jones
ISBN #978-1-957488-21-9

Second Edition

Great Publishing Company

Benai Emunah Institute
121 Mountain Way Drive, Kerrville, Texas 78028   830-257-7414